C·O·T·T·A·G·E
CROSS-STITCH

20 DESIGNS CELEBRATING THE SIMPLE JOYS OF HOME

T0286829

GAIL BUSSI

STACKPOLE BOOKS

Essex, Connecticut
Blue Ridge Summit, Pennsylvania

STACKPOLE BOOKS

An imprint of Globe Pequot, the trade division of
The Rowman & Littlefield Publishing Group, Inc.
4501 Forbes Blvd., Ste. 200
Lanham, MD 20706
www.rowman.com

Distributed by NATIONAL BOOK NETWORK
800-462-6420

British Library Cataloguing in Publication Information available

Library of Congress Cataloging-in-Publication Data

Names: Bussi, Gail, author.
Title: Cottage cross-stitch / Gail Bussi.
Description: Essex, Connecticut : Stackpole Books, [2024] | Summary: "If you daydream of a simple life in a little house on a hill or near the sea, this book is full of designs that will inspire and feed your love of all things homey and sweet. The 20 stitchings feature a variety of tiny homes and the relaxing rituals of cottage living. Each project includes chart, finished photo, materials, and full instructions"—Provided by publisher.
Identifiers: LCCN 2023039144 (print) | LCCN 2023039145 (ebook) | ISBN 9780811773591 (paperback) | ISBN 9780811773607 (epub)
Subjects: LCSH: Cross-stitch—Patterns. | Cottages—Miscellanea.
Classification: LCC TT778.C76 B875 2024 (print) | LCC TT778.C76 (ebook) | DDC 746.44/3041.—dc23/eng/20231220
LC record available at https://lccn.loc.gov/2023039144
LC ebook record available at https://lccn.loc.gov/2023039145

First Edition

For all those who have supported my design and stitching over the years, especially my late mom, who was the most creative person I know! For the team at Stackpole Books, for giving me another great opportunity! And for my dear friend Don—thanks for doing such a great job with the photos!

CONTENTS

INTRODUCTION

The word *cottage* means different things to all of us, depending on our background, country of origin, and so on—but I believe we all see cottages as a symbol of warmth, comfort, and simple everyday pleasures. Plus, they are just so cute and appealing!

These days, partly in response to the difficult times we have all experienced since the pandemic of early 2020, there has been an enormous resurgence of interest in going back to a more simple and peaceful way of life, and the "cottage core" aesthetic is linked to that desire on many levels. This book contains 20 cottage-themed designs aimed at cross-stitchers of all skill levels. More than that, it's a book that will, ideally, remind us all just how beautiful a simple life at home can be!

BASIC INSTRUCTIONS

All the designs in this book are relatively simple and quick to stitch—within the reach of a beginning stitcher, once you have the basics down. Cross-stitch, backstitch, and French knots are the basic stitches used throughout, with a few half stitches where necessary.

I stitch my designs on evenweave or linen fabrics, because I prefer the look of the finished pieces, but many stitchers prefer to use Aida, and that is certainly possible with these designs, although you may have to change the suggested colors.

DMC floss has been used to stitch these projects; its quality is excellent and the range of colors so vast! I do like overdyed threads, which give subtle shading to stitches, but I am aware that a particular range of overdyed threads might not be available to all stitchers, and there are also cost implications. However, if you want to try different threads, go for it—the important thing is to make your stitching your own!

Other things to know:

- Two strands of embroidery floss are used for cross-stitches, while one is used for backstitch. French knots are made with one strand of floss, wrapped twice around the needle.
- You will need size 24 or 26 tapestry/cross-stitch needles to stitch these projects, as well as a pair of small, sharp embroidery scissors.
- For finishing some of the designs, you will need larger dressmaking scissors, pins, and suitable cotton sewing thread (as well as a steam iron for pressing the finished projects). A sewing machine is useful when stitching some projects (like little pillows), but it is definitely not essential, and all the projects in this book can also be finished with hand sewing.

STITCHES

Full Cross-Stitch

Cross-stitch can be worked as a counted stitch over a single square on Aida fabric (shown here) or over two threads when using an evenweave fabric. Each stitch comprises two diagonal stitches that cross in the center. They can be worked individually or in vertical and horizontal rows. Keep the stitches uniform by making sure the top stitch always crosses in the same direction, from upper left to lower right.

Half Cross-Stitch

Partial cross-stitches may be used where colors abut or along the edges of a design. For a half stitch, work one full diagonal across the square (half the cross).

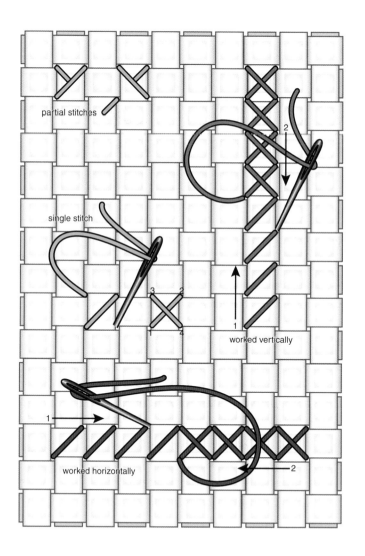

Illustrations and instructions for stitches excerpted from Embroidery Basics *by Cheryl Fall © 2013 by Stackpole Books. Used with permission.*

Backstitch

Backstitch is used to outline a shape and is worked in a motion of two steps forward and one step back. To work the stitch, bring the needle up through the fabric a stitch length's distance from the starting point and insert the needle at the starting point, working the stitch backward. Bring the needle up again a stitch length's distance from the first stitch, and continue working in this manner to the end.

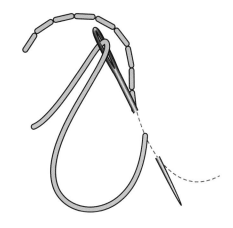

Petite Stitch

A petite stitch is a ¼-size full cross-stitch worked into one of the corners of a square.

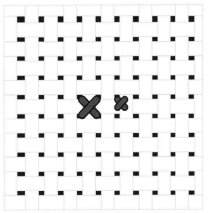

French Knot

Bring the needle up through the fabric and wrap the working thread around the needle twice. Insert the needle back into the fabric very close to (but not in) the same hole you came out of, and pull the thread through, guiding it with your opposite hand as it passes through the fabric. Do not wrap too tightly, or you'll have a difficult time pulling the needle through the knot. The thread should be against the needle, but not snug or tight. If your knot pulls through to the other side when working the stitch, try loosening the wrap a bit and make sure you're not going down into the same hole. You will need a bridge to hold the knot on the surface; usually a fiber or two in the fabric will suffice.

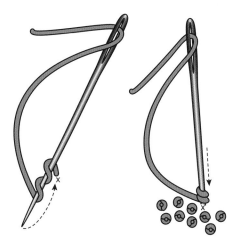

Cottage Comforts

This collection of cottage-themed pieces features some traditional (and not so traditional) homes: samplers and other ideas for celebrating cottage life, such as cottage kitchens and recipes, little houses by the sea, living in a vintage van, and more! These designs would make lovely decorative accents for the home or a very special gift, and none are particularly difficult to do or overly large in size.

Cottage Garden Quilt

It's hard to imagine a beautiful cottage without a lovely, fragrant garden surrounding it—a colorful, tranquil place filled with traditional flowers like roses, daisies, sweet peas, daffodils, forget-me-nots, and marigolds. This pattern, designed to resemble a quilt patch, reminds us of this gentle beauty with its rows of bright floral patterns. I have finished it here as a small cushion, but, if desired, it could also be turned into a framed piece.

Fabric: 28-count water lily Jobelan by Wichelt (stitched over 2 threads)
Stitch count: 97 wide × 97 high
Approx. stitched size: 6½ × 6½ in. (16.5 × 16.5 cm)

Cut fabric to measure at least 10 inches (25.5 cm) square, and then fold in half and count out to find a suitable place to start stitching. When stitching is completed, wash and lightly press the piece. Trim to within 1¾ inch (4.5 cm) of the stitching area (this includes a ½-inch/1.25-cm seam). Cut a piece of suitable cotton patchwork fabric to measure the same size, and pin the two pieces together, right sides facing. Stitch together, leaving a 3-inch (7.5-cm) opening on one side. Turn to the right side and lightly stuff with fiberfill before slip-stitching the opening closed.

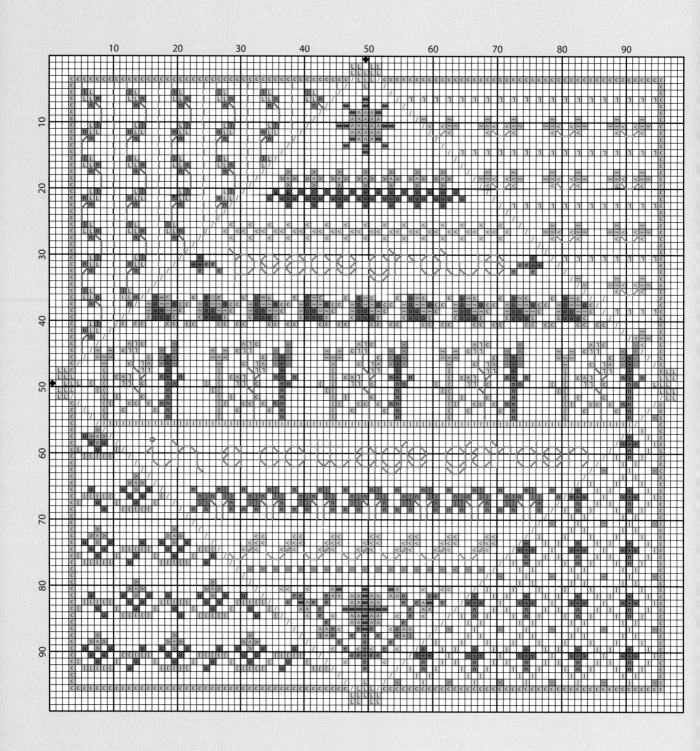

Floss Used for Full Stitches:

	Symbol	Strands	Type	Number	Color
	o	2	DMC	223	Shell Pink-LT
	~	2	DMC	224	Shell Pink-VY LT
	)	2	DMC	316	Antique Mauve-MD
	u	2	DMC	320	Pistachio Green-MD
	(	2	DMC	368	Pistachio Green-LT
	1	2	DMC	436	Tan
	n	2	DMC	522	Fern Green
	I	2	DMC	524	Fern Green-VY LT
	^	2	DMC	676	Old Gold-LT
	⊗	2	DMC	729	Old Gold-MD
	L	2	DMC	778	Antique Mauve-VY LT
	/	2	DMC	822	Beige Gray-LT
	>	2	DMC	932	Antique Blue-LT
	e	2	DMC	3012	Khaki Green-MD
	<	2	DMC	3013	Khaki Green-LT
	+	2	DMC	3041	Antique Violet-MD
	-	2	DMC	3042	Antique Violet-LT
	c	2	DMC	3053	Green Gray
	˥	2	DMC	3752	Antique Blue-VY LT

Floss Used for French Knots:

	Symbol	Strands	Type	Number	Color
	●	1	DMC	3790	Beige Gray-UL DK

Floss Used for Back Stitches:

	Symbol	Strands	Type	Number	Color
	▬	1	DMC	223	Shell Pink-LT
	▬	1	DMC	522	Fern Green
	▬	1	DMC	3012	Khaki Green-MD
	▬	1	DMC	3363	Pine Green-MD
	▬	1	DMC	3790	Beige Gray-UL DK

Apple Crisp Cake

No cottage would be complete without an apple tree, yielding fragrant blossoms in spring and a harvest of delicious fruit in summer and fall. This stitched recipe sampler is both colorful and practical and would make a sweet gift for a food-loving friend.

Fabric: 28-count lambswool Jobelan by Wichelt (stitched over 2 threads)
Stitch count: 63 wide × 99 high
Approx. stitched size: 4½ × 7¼ in. (11.5 × 18.5 cm)

Cut fabric to measure at least 8 × 11 inches (20.5 × 28 cm), and then fold in half and count out to start stitching at a suitable place. When stitching is complete, wash and press lightly. Cut a piece of backing board to measure 6 × 8 inches (15 × 20.5 cm), and then fold the stitched piece over the backing board, trimming if necessary. Center it on the board and hold it in place on the back with double-sided tape or glue.

Cut a larger piece of backing board to measure approximately 7½ × 9½ inches (19 × 24 cm) and cover with suitable cotton fabric, folding and gluing it in place on the back. Center the stitched piece on the fabric backing board and glue in place, as shown in the picture.

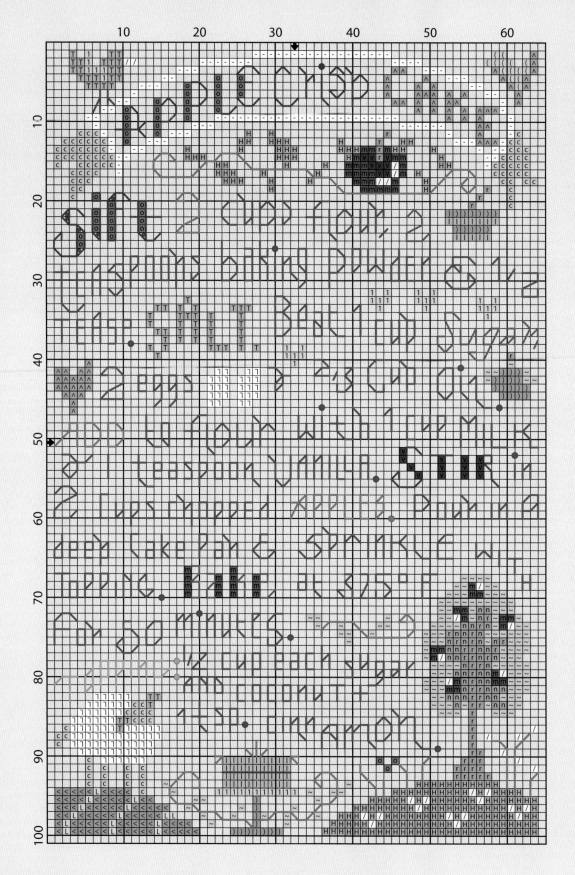

Floss Used for Full Stitches:

Symbol		Strands	Type	Number	Color
	n	2	DMC	320	Pistachio Green-MD
	V	2	DMC	347	Salmon-VY DK
	)	2	DMC	352	Coral-LT
	1	2	DMC	353	Peach
	~	2	DMC	368	Pistachio Green-LT
	I	2	DMC	436	Tan
	T	2	DMC	642	Beige Gray-DK
	c	2	DMC	644	Beige Gray-MD
	^	2	DMC	760	Salmon
	(	2	DMC	761	Salmon-LT
	-	2	DMC	822	Beige Gray-LT
	m	2	DMC	3328	Salmon-DK
	<	2	DMC	3347	Yellow Green-MD
	L	2	DMC	3348	Yellow Green-LT
	H	2	DMC	3364	Pine Green
	o	2	DMC	3712	Salmon-MD
	/	2	DMC	3855	Autumn Gold-LT
	r	2	DMC	3863	Mocha Beige-MD
	1	2	DMC	3865	Winter White

Floss Used for Quarter Stitches:

Symbol		Strands	Type	Number	Color
	o	2	DMC	3712	Salmon-MD

Floss Used for French Knots:

Symbol		Strands	Type	Number	Color
	●	1	DMC	347	Salmon-VY DK
	●	1	DMC	352	Coral-LT
	●	1	DMC	3363	Pine Green-MD
	●	1	DMC	3790	Beige Gray-UL DK

Floss Used for Back Stitches:

Symbol		Strands	Type	Number	Color
	——	1	DMC	347	Salmon-VY DK
	——	1	DMC	352	Coral-LT
	——	1	DMC	3328	Salmon-DK
	——	1	DMC	3363	Pine Green-MD
	——	1	DMC	3790	Beige Gray-UL DK

"The real magic in a kitchen doesn't lie in the food . . .
it lies in the cook."

Anonymous

My Cottage Kitchen

When we think about cottages, a lovely and cozy kitchen is probably the first thing that comes to mind, full of delicious things like herbs on the windowsill, bowls of fresh lemons and eggs, bright jars of preserves, and the delicious aroma of just-baked cakes and pies! I have tried to capture this simple charm in this easy-to-stitch and colorful sampler.

Our kitchens are also absolutely bursting with all kinds of natural magic, particularly when it comes to the herbs and spices we use, whether fresh or dried. For example, cinnamon is for prosperity, rosemary is for healing and love, sage is for wisdom, lemon is for positive vibes, parsley is for protection, mint is for cleansing, orange is for vitality and energy, and vanilla is for passion!

Fabric: 28-count antique white Jobelan by Wichelt (stitched over 2 threads)
Stitch count: 97 wide × 73 high
Approx. stitched size: 7 × 5¼ in. (18 × 13.5 cm)

Cut fabric to measure at least 8 × 11 inches (20.5 × 28 cm), and then fold and count out from the center to start stitching at a suitable point. When stitching is complete, wash and lightly press the work. This piece was inserted into an antique blue frame measuring 9½ × 7½ inches (24 × 19 cm) and stretched over a backing board to fit into the frame.

Floss Used for Full Stitches:

Symbol		Strands	Type	Number	Color
	⟨	2	DMC	159	Gray Blue-LT
	∧	2	DMC	160	Gray Blue-MD
	L	2	DMC	437	Tan-LT
	H	2	DMC	522	Fern Green
	I	2	DMC	524	Fern Green-VY LT
	v	2	DMC	644	Beige Gray-MD
	↑	2	DMC	648	Beaver Gray-LT
	·	2	DMC	727	Topaz-VY LT
	u	2	DMC	738	Tan-VY LT
	0	2	DMC	745	Yellow-LT Pale
	)	2	DMC	758	Terra Cotta-VY LT
	o	2	DMC	760	Salmon
	/	2	DMC	761	Salmon-LT
	-	2	DMC	822	Beige Gray-LT
	T	2	DMC	841	Beige Brown-LT
	<	2	DMC	3012	Khaki Green-MD
	~	2	DMC	3072	Beaver Gray-VY LT
	●●	2	DMC	3363	Pine Green-MD
	r	2	DMC	3364	Pine Green
	n	2	DMC	3712	Salmon-MD
	>	2	DMC	3713	Salmon-VY LT
	1	2	DMC	3778	Terra Cotta-LT
	c	2	DMC	3855	Autumn Gold-LT
	∞	2	DMC	3863	Mocha Beige-MD
	⌐	2	DMC	3865	Winter White

Floss Used for Half Stitches:

Symbol		Strands	Type	Number	Color
	﹩	2	DMC	413	Pewter Gray-DK

Floss Used for French Knots:

Symbol		Strands	Type	Number	Color
	●	1	DMC	161	Gray Blue

Floss Used for Back Stitches:

Symbol		Strands	Type	Number	Color
	━━━	1	DMC	161	Gray Blue
	━━━	1	DMC	413	Pewter Gray-DK
	━━━	1	DMC	3363	Pine Green-MD
	━━━	1	DMC	3863	Mocha Beige-MD

14

Wool and Whimsy Cottage

This is a larger but still simple-to-stitch piece, featuring a little cottage wool store flanked by two cute sheep (who presumably supply the wool for the shop!). Aspects of the design could also be stitched separately. For example, the cottage could be stitched as a standalone piece, or the sheep could be stitched on small, decorative pillows.

Fabric: 28-count lambswool Jobelan by Wichelt (stitched over 2 threads)
Stitch count: 131 wide × 71 high
Approx. stitched size: 8¼ × 4½ in. (21 × 11.5 cm)

Cut fabric to measure at least 9 × 12 inches (23 × 30.5 cm), and then fold in half and count out to start stitching at a suitable point. When stitching is complete, wash and press lightly. Cut a piece of backing board measuring 9½ × 5½ inches (24 × 14 cm), and cut the stitched piece to measure about 2 inches (5 cm) larger all around. Stretch over the backing board, ensuring that it is centered, and then hold in place on the back with double-sided tape or glue. If desired, make a ribbon bow and glue it to the top center of the piece, holding it in place with several large pins.

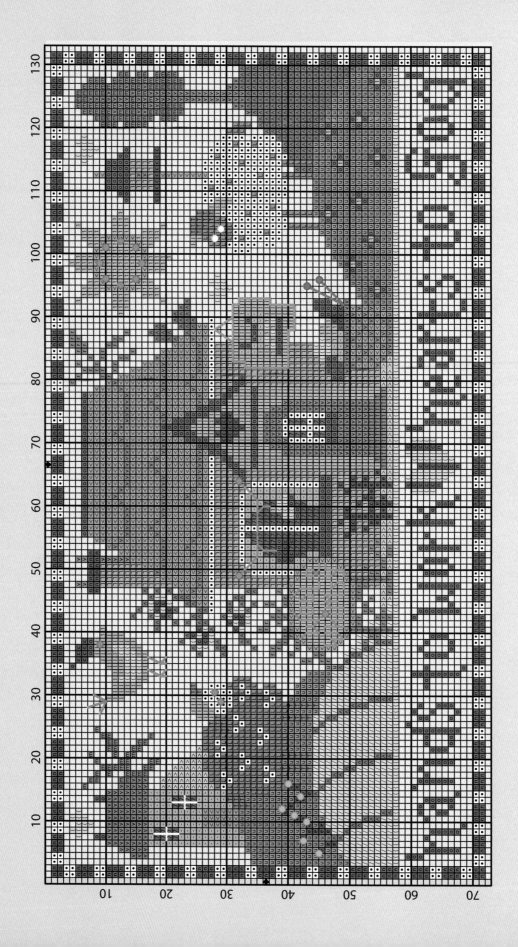

Floss Used for Full Stitches:

	Symbol	Strands	Type	Number	Color
	m	2	DMC	368	Pistachio Green-LT
	7	2	DMC	414	Steel Gray-DK
	∧	2	DMC	522	Fern Green
	/	2	DMC	524	Fern Green-VY LT
	<	2	DMC	613	Drab Brown-VY LT
	T	2	DMC	640	Beige Gray-VY DK
	L	2	DMC	642	Beige Gray-DK
	I	2	DMC	644	Beige Gray-MD
	1	2	DMC	676	Old Gold-LT
	o	2	DMC	926	Gray Green-MD
	-	2	DMC	927	Gray Green-LT
	r	2	DMC	3012	Khaki Green-MD
	>	2	DMC	3013	Khaki Green-LT
	e	2	DMC	3363	Pine Green-MD
	u	2	DMC	3364	Pine Green
	c	2	DMC	3778	Terra Cotta-LT
	[(	2	DMC	3779	Terra Cotta-UL VY LT
	n	2	DMC	3859	Rosewood-LT
	v	2	DMC	3863	Mocha Beige-MD
	⌐	2	DMC	3864	Mocha Beige-LT
	·	2	DMC	3865	Winter White

Floss Used for French Knots:

	Symbol	Strands	Type	Number	Color
	●	1	DMC	414	Steel Gray-DK
	●	1	DMC	640	Beige Gray-VY DK
	●	1	DMC	676	Old Gold-LT
	○	1	DMC	3865	Winter White

Floss Used for Back Stitches:

	Symbol	Strands	Type	Number	Color
	▬▬	1	DMC	414	Steel Gray-DK
	───	1	DMC	640	Beige Gray-VY DK
	───	1	DMC	3865	Winter White

"Where we love is home, home
that our feet may leave,
but not our hearts . . ."
Oliver Wendell Holmes

ronstik/iStock/Getty Images Plus via Getty Images

To bring the gentle fragrance of a cottage garden into your home, try making this floral room/linen spray: Place 1 cup of distilled water in a small spray bottle, and then add 2 tablespoons vodka (the vodka acts as a preservative). Add 3 drops each of rose, lavender, and bergamot essential oils, and shake well. You can spray this mist lightly into the air or spray a little onto bedlinens before ironing them for a delicate touch of floral freshness.

Little House on Wheels

Cottages and little houses can take many forms, and some of them take us from place to place. I know several people who not only travel but also live full time in vintage vans or RVs, and they have turned these vehicles into truly delightful cottage spaces. In fact, I have a dream of one day creating my own little home on wheels—making it a traveling art studio and tea shop—and this design came about because of that dream!

Fabric: 32-count antique white Jobelan by Wichelt (stitched over 2 threads)
Stitch count: 95 wide × 67 high
Approx. stitched size: 6 × 4¼ in. (15 × 11 cm)

Cut fabric to measure at least 10 × 8 inches (25.5 × 20.5cm), and then fold in half and count out to start stitching at a suitable point. When stitching is complete, wash and lightly press the work. Cut a piece of foam core board to measure 8 × 6 inches (20.5 × 15 cm), and then stretch the stitching evenly over the board and hold in place at the back with double-sided tape or glue. Cut another piece of board to measure approximately 9¼ × 7¼ inches (23.5 × 18.5 cm) and cover with suitable cotton fabric, folding the fabric to the back and gluing it in place. Place the stitched piece centered on the backing board and glue firmly in place, as per the photo.

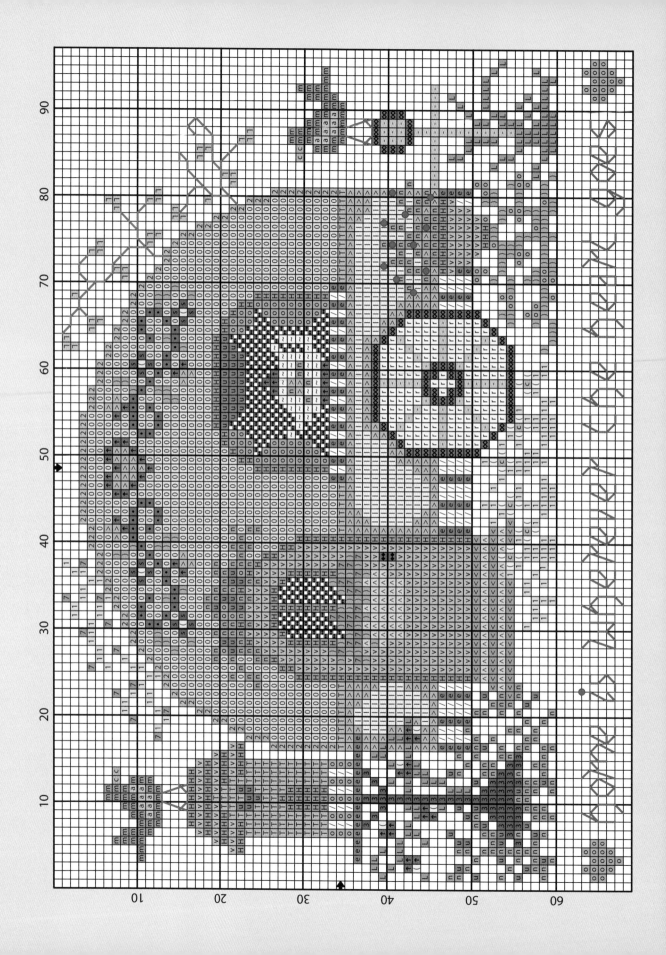

Floss Used for Full Stitches:

	Symbol	Strands	Type	Number	Color
	0	2	DMC	02	Lightest Gray
	2	2	DMC	03	Med Lightest Gray
	↑	2	DMC	223	Shell Pink-LT
	>	2	DMC	224	Shell Pink-VY LT
	I	2	DMC	225	Shell Pink-UL VY LT
	u	2	DMC	316	Antique Mauve-MD
	a	2	DMC	353	Peach
	◆◆	2	DMC	414	Steel Gray-DK
	<	2	DMC	436	Tan
	∧	2	DMC	437	Tan-LT
	n	2	DMC	522	Fern Green
	⌐	2	DMC	523	Fern Green-LT
	3	2	DMC	611	Drab Brown
	m	2	DMC	642	Beige Gray-DK
	∞	2	DMC	646	Beaver Gray-DK
	-	2	DMC	648	Beaver Gray-LT
	~	2	DMC	822	Beige Gray-LT
	e	2	DMC	926	Gray Green-MD
	T	2	DMC	927	Gray Green-LT
	L	2	DMC	3012	Khaki Green-MD
	1	2	DMC	3013	Khaki Green-LT
	H	2	DMC	3032	Mocha Brown-MD
	s	2	DMC	3041	Antique Violet-MD
	7	2	DMC	3042	Antique Violet-LT
	r	2	DMC	3072	Beaver Gray-VY LT
	·	2	DMC	3363	Pine Green-MD
	)	2	DMC	3364	Pine Green
	o	2	DMC	3727	Antique Mauve-LT
	v	2	DMC	3782	Mocha Brown-LT
	c	2	DMC	3827	Golden Brown-Pale
	(	2	DMC	3855	Autumn Gold-LT
	/	2	DMC	3865	Winter White

Floss Used for Half Stitches:

	Symbol	Strands	Type	Number	Color
	◆◆	2	DMC	414	Steel Gray-DK

Floss Used for French Knots:

	Symbol	Strands	Type	Number	Color
	●	1	DMC	3041	Antique Violet-MD
	●	1	DMC	3768	Gray Green-DK

Floss Used for Back Stitches:

	Symbol	Strands	Type	Number	Color
	▬▬▬	1	DMC	611	Drab Brown
	▬▬▬	1	DMC	3363	Pine Green-MD
	▬▬▬	1	DMC	3768	Gray Green-DK

Cottage Cakery

When I think of cottages, I always imagine them with a steady supply of delicious home-baked cakes, a reminder of the sweetness of life! This delicious design is a snap to stitch and will look good in any little house.

Fabric: 28-count antique white Jobelan by Wichelt (stitched over two threads)
Stitch count: 99 wide × 57 high
Approx. stitched size: 7 × 4 in. (18 × 10 cm)

Cut fabric to measure at least 11 × 7 inches (28 × 18 cm), and then fold in half and count out to start stitching at a suitable point. When stitching is complete, wash and lightly press the piece. This design is shown unfinished and flat here in the book, but there are a number of finishing options: it would look good framed or stitched up as a small, rectangular pillow.

25

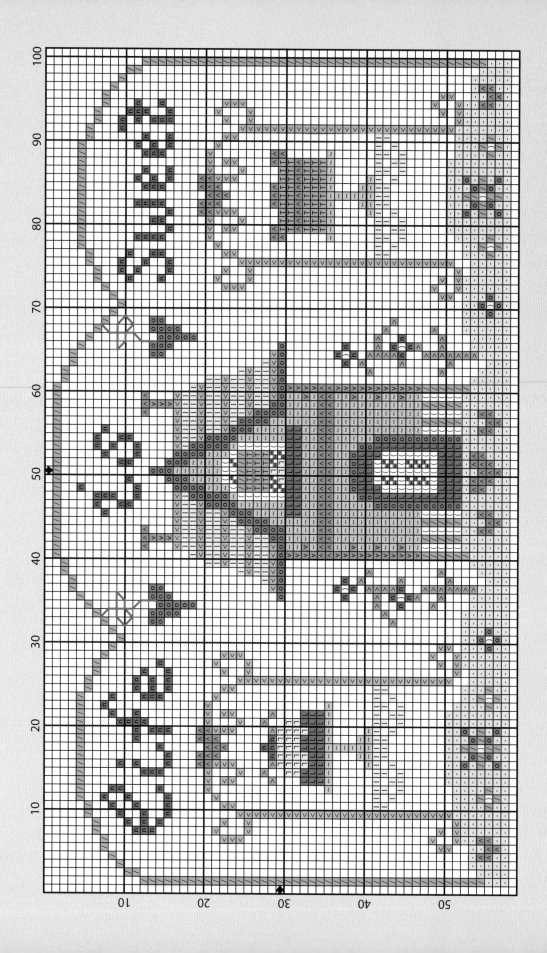

Floss Used for Full Stitches:

Symbol		Strands	Type	Number	Color
	I	2	DMC	02	Lightest Gray
	<	2	DMC	03	Med Lightest Gray
	^	2	DMC	152	Shell Pink-MD LT
	n	2	DMC	223	Shell Pink-LT
	⅂	2	DMC	225	Shell Pink-UL VY LT
	o	2	DMC	316	Antique Mauve-MD
	T	2	DMC	436	Tan
	>	2	DMC	522	Fern Green
	-	2	DMC	524	Fern Green-VY LT
	L	2	DMC	840	Beige Brown-MD
	v	2	DMC	841	Beige Brown-LT
	~	2	DMC	842	Beige Brown-VY LT
	/	2	DMC	3727	Antique Mauve-LT
	)	2	DMC	3855	Autumn Gold-LT
	(	2	DMC	3865	Winter White

Floss Used for Half Stitches:

Symbol		Strands	Type	Number	Color
	••	2	DMC	414	Steel Gray-DK

Floss Used for Back Stitches:

Symbol		Strands	Type	Number	Color
	▬▬▬	1	DMC	316	Antique Mauve-MD
	▬▬▬	1	DMC	840	Beige Brown-MD

"A house is not beautiful because of its walls, a house is beautiful because of its cakes."

Russian proverb

A Cottage Stitching Journal

Stitching of all kinds—embroidery, patchwork, cross-stitch, and more—is so typical of cottage décor, lending a handmade warmth and comfort to our homes. This whimsical design celebrates the many gifts that stitching brings to us.

Fabric: 28-count water lily Jobelan by Wichelt (stitched over 2 threads)
Stitch count: 61 wide × 103 high
Approx. stitched size: 4¼ × 7½ in. (11 × 19 cm)

Cut fabric at least 7 × 11 inches (18 × 28 cm), and then fold in half and count out to start stitching at a suitable point. When stitching is complete, wash and press lightly, and then finish the piece as desired. This design is shown flat and unfinished, but it could be framed in a traditional sampler style or used to cover a stitching journal or similar book. (Please note that you will need five tiny buttons [¼ inch/0.5 cm] to finish the piece as shown; alternatively, you could work large French knots in their place.)

Floss Used for Full Stitches:

Symbol		Strands	Type	Number	Color
	<	2	DMC	152	Shell Pink-MD LT
	o	2	DMC	223	Shell Pink-LT
	/	2	DMC	225	Shell Pink-UL VY LT
	c	2	DMC	316	Antique Mauve-MD
	◆◆	2	DMC	414	Steel Gray-DK
	ʌ	2	DMC	522	Fern Green
	)	2	DMC	523	Fern Green-LT
	I	2	DMC	642	Beige Gray-DK
	v	2	DMC	644	Beige Gray-MD
	1	2	DMC	676	Old Gold-LT
	~	2	DMC	738	Tan-VY LT
	·	2	DMC	822	Beige Gray-LT
	n	2	DMC	926	Gray Green-MD
	L	2	DMC	3041	Antique Violet-MD
	-	2	DMC	3042	Antique Violet-LT
	u	2	DMC	3364	Pine Green
	(	2	DMC	3727	Antique Mauve-LT

Floss Used for French Knots:

Symbol		Strands	Type	Number	Color
	●	1	DMC	3726	Antique Mauve-DK

Floss Used for Back Stitches:

Symbol		Strands	Type	Number	Color
	——	1	DMC	152	Shell Pink-MD LT
	——	1	DMC	223	Shell Pink-LT
	——	1	DMC	414	Steel Gray-DK
	——	1	DMC	644	Beige Gray-MD
	——	1	DMC	926	Gray Green-MD
	——	1	DMC	3041	Antique Violet-MD
	——	1	DMC	3042	Antique Violet-LT
	——	1	DMC	3363	Pine Green-MD
	——	1	DMC	3726	Antique Mauve-DK

Floss Used for Specialty Stitches:

Symbol		Strands	Type	Number	Color
Four-Sided		2	DMC	152	Shell Pink-MD LT

House by the Sea

There's a kind of collective nostalgia for houses by the sea that are within sight and sound of the surf and filled with ocean magic. I am extremely fortunate to live in such a little house, and it was the inspiration for this small, easy-to-stitch design. It would make a great gift for a beach cottage, too. Even if you don't live near the sea, you can add a touch of beach magic by arranging some beautiful shells in a shallow basket and placing a small bottle of seawater next to them. Sprinkle a little of the water around your living room when you need to introduce some fresh and positive energy to your home.

Fabric: 32-count café mocha Country French Linen by Wichelt (stitched over two threads)
Stitch count: 71 wide × 39 high
Approx. stitched size: 4¼ × 2½ in. (11 × 6.5 cm)

Cut fabric to measure at least 8 × 5 inches (20.5 × 13 cm), and then fold in half and count out to start stitching at a suitable point. When stitching is complete, wash and lightly press the piece. This design was framed in a little antique blue frame with an aperture measuring 5¼ × 3½ inches (13.5 × 9 cm); it was stretched over a piece of backing board to fit the aperture and held in place on the back with double-sided tape before being inserted into the frame.

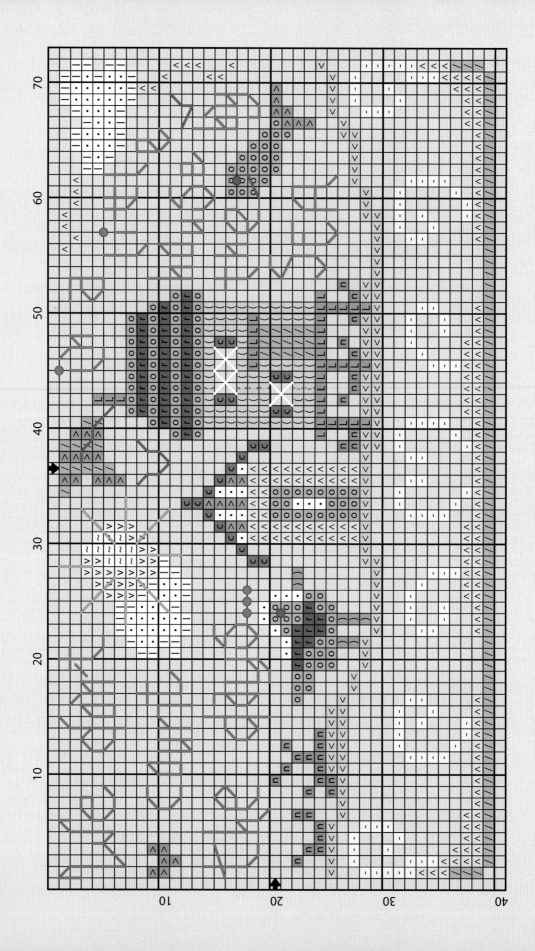

Floss Used for Full Stitches:

Symbol		Strands	Type	Number	Color
■	r	2	DMC	317	Pewter Gray
■	o	2	DMC	415	Pearl Gray
□	<	2	DMC	422	Hazelnut Brown-LT
□	~	2	DMC	677	Old Gold-VY LT
■	((	2	DMC	738	Tan-VY LT
■	>	2	DMC	760	Salmon
■	c	2	DMC	931	Antique Blue-MD
■	/	2	DMC	932	Antique Blue-LT
■	n	2	DMC	3012	Khaki Green-MD
□	I	2	DMC	3072	Beaver Gray-VY LT
■	^	2	DMC	3752	Antique Blue-VY LT
□	-	2	DMC	3753	Antique Blue-UL VY LT
■	))	2	DMC	3827	Golden Brown-Pale
□	v	2	DMC	3855	Autumn Gold-LT
■	L	2	DMC	3863	Mocha Beige-MD
□	·	2	DMC	White	White

Floss Used for French Knots:

Symbol		Strands	Type	Number	Color
■	●	1	DMC	317	Pewter Gray
■	●	1	DMC	931	Antique Blue-MD

Floss Used for Back Stitches:

Symbol		Strands	Type	Number	Color
■	▬▬▬	1	DMC	317	Pewter Gray
■	▬▬▬	1	DMC	931	Antique Blue-MD
■	▬▬▬	1	DMC	3827	Golden Brown-Pale
□	▬▬▬	1	DMC	White	White

Cottage Spirit

Though our visions of the ideal cottage may differ, a "cottage" ultimately represents home in its best and most beautiful sense, and the pretty designs in this section are themed around this feeling of happiness and belonging, including some lovely quotes about home, family, and everyday blessings.

Cottage Joy Mandala

Mandalas are a unique and beautiful way of representing soul and spirit, and this design was created to honor the spirit of the home and the shelter it gives us on every level. This is an easy-to-stitch piece and would also make a wonderful housewarming gift!

Fabric: 28-count antique white Jobelan by Wichelt (stitched over two threads)
Stitch count: 55 wide × 55 high
Approx. stitched size: 4 in. (10 cm) in diameter

Cut fabric to measure at least 7 inches (18 cm) in diameter, and then fold in half and count out to start stitching at a suitable point. After stitching is complete, wash and lightly press the piece; cut a piece of cotton backing fabric the same size, and then place the stitched piece and backing fabric in a 6-inch (15 cm) wooden hoop, making sure the stitching is centered. Tighten the hoop and trim the fabric all round. Add ribbon for hanging.

Floss Used for Full Stitches:

Symbol		Strands	Type	Number	Color
	/	2	DMC	25	Palest Mauve
	<	2	DMC	30	Violet-Blue
	n	2	DMC	368	Pistachio Green-LT
	)	2	DMC	676	Old Gold-LT
	ʌ	2	DMC	962	Dusty Rose-MD
	(	2	DMC	963	Dusty Rose-UL VY LT
	o	2	DMC	3022	Brown Gray-MD
	>	2	DMC	3024	Brown Gray-VY LT
	v	2	DMC	3032	Mocha Brown-MD
	⌐	2	DMC	3047	Yellow Beige-LT
	-	2	DMC	3053	Green Gray
	I	2	DMC	3836	Grape-LT
	~	2	DMC	26	Pale Mauve

Floss Used for Half Stitches:

Symbol		Strands	Type	Number	Color
	⊠	2	DMC	414	Steel Gray-DK

"The ideal of happiness has always taken material form in the home, whether cottage or castle."

Simone de Beauvoir

44

Little House . . .

"A small house can hold as much love as a large one." This anonymous quote is so true, and it was the inspiration for this design, with its pretty cottage and soft colors. Hang it on your wall to remind yourself of this gentle truth or stitch it as a gift for someone in their new home.

Fabric: 28-count china pearl Jobelan by Wichelt (stitched over two threads)
Stitch count: 85 wide × 85 high
Approx. stitched size: 6 in. (15 cm) in diameter

Cut fabric to measure at least 10 inches (25.5 cm) in diameter, and then fold in half and count out to start stitching at a suitable point. When stitching is finished, wash and press lightly. Cut a piece of cotton backing fabric the same size and insert the stitched piece/backing fabric into an 8-inch (20.5-cm) wooden hoop. Make sure the design is centered in the hoop, and then tighten the screws and trim excess fabric around the edges (or fold it back and glue it out of sight). Attach a ribbon for hanging.

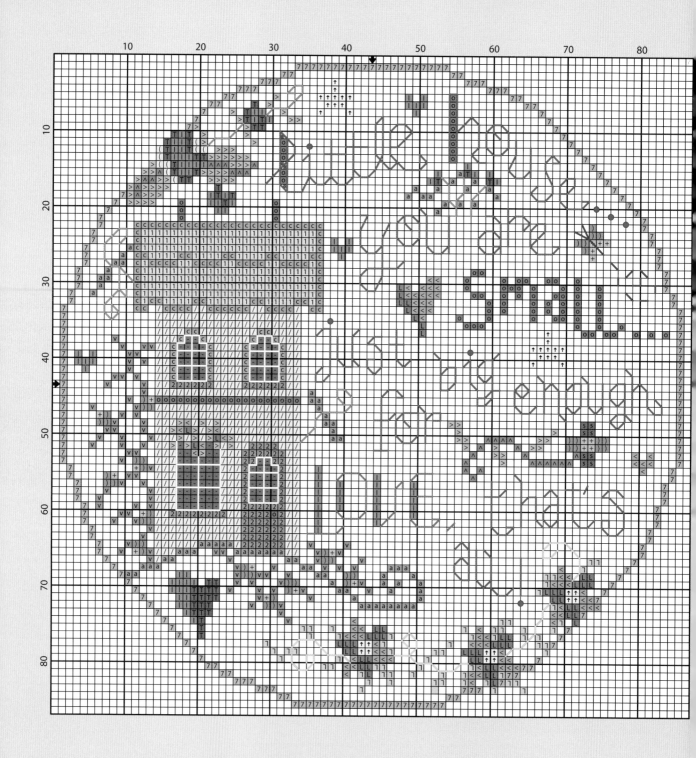

Floss Used for Full Stitches:

Symbol		Strands	Type	Number	Color
	I	2	DMC	152	Shell Pink-MD LT
	T	2	DMC	223	Shell Pink-LT
	((	2	DMC	225	Shell Pink-UL VY LT
	L	2	DMC	316	Antique Mauve-MD
	-	2	DMC	414	Steel Gray-DK
	a	2	DMC	522	Fern Green
	c	2	DMC	642	Beige Gray-DK
	1	2	DMC	644	Beige Gray-MD
	+	2	DMC	676	Old Gold-LT
	o	2	DMC	926	Gray Green-MD
	7	2	DMC	927	Gray Green-LT
	/	2	DMC	928	Gray Green-VY LT
	V	2	DMC	3012	Khaki Green-MD
	7	2	DMC	3013	Khaki Green-LT
	s	2	DMC	3041	Antique Violet-MD
	)	2	DMC	3042	Antique Violet-LT
	^	2	DMC	3363	Pine Green-MD
	>	2	DMC	3364	Pine Green
	<	2	DMC	3727	Antique Mauve-LT
	↑	2	DMC	3855	Autumn Gold-LT
	2	2	DMC	3863	Mocha Beige-MD

Floss Used for Quarter Stitches:

Symbol		Strands	Type	Number	Color
	o	2	DMC	926	Gray Green-MD

Floss Used for French Knots:

Symbol		Strands	Type	Number	Color
	●	1	DMC	3768	Gray Green-DK

Floss Used for Back Stitches:

Symbol		Strands	Type	Number	Color
		1	DMC	223	Shell Pink-LT
		1	DMC	3013	Khaki Green-LT
		1	DMC	3363	Pine Green-MD
		1	DMC	3768	Gray Green-DK
		1	DMC	3790	Beige Gray-UL DK
		1	DMC	3865	Winter White

48

Welcome Home

This is a little traditional-style sampler done in shades of blue. Blue is such a perfect cottage color, and this design makes me think of my Great-Aunt Emily's kitchen, with its dresser filled with antique blue-and-white china and a blue glass jug filled with daisies!

Fabric: 28-count antique white Jobelan by Wichelt (stitched over 2 threads)
Stitch count: 55 wide × 83 high
Approx. stitched size: 4 × 6 in. (10 × 15 cm)

Cut fabric to measure at least 8 × 10 inches (20.5 × 25.5 cm), and then fold in half and count out to start stitching at a suitable point. When stitching is complete, wash and press lightly. This piece was finished in a whitewashed antique frame measuring 5¼ × 7¼ inches (13.5 × 18.5 cm). It was centered and stretched over a backing board and held in place with double-sided tape before being inserted into the frame.

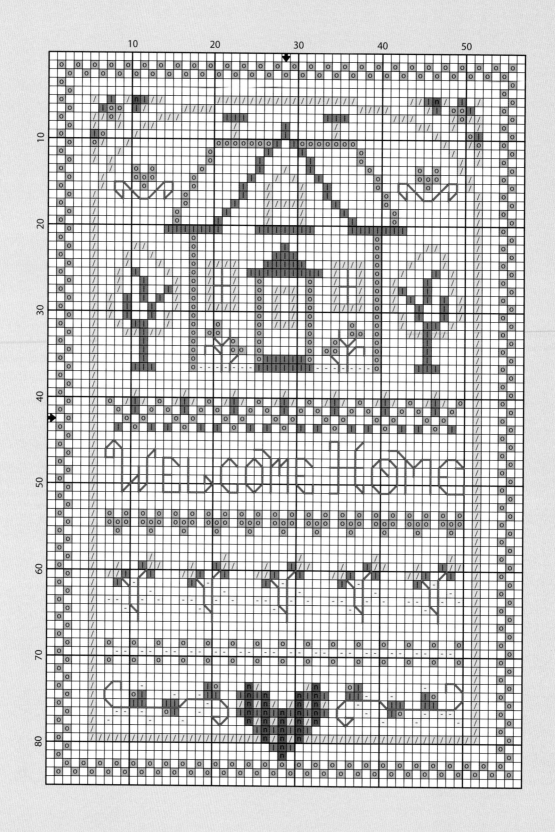

Floss Used for Full Stitches:

Symbol		Strands	Type	Number	Color
■	n	2	DMC	930	Antique Blue-DK
■	l	2	DMC	931	Antique Blue-MD
■	o	2	DMC	932	Antique Blue-LT
□	/	2	DMC	3752	Antique Blue-VY LT
□	-	2	DMC	3753	Antique Blue-UL VY LT

Floss Used for Back Stitches:

Symbol		Strands	Type	Number	Color
■	———	1	DMC	930	Antique Blue-DK

Andy Hook/Moment via Getty Images

Janna Danilova/iStock/Getty Images Plus via Getty Images

Nothing says "welcome home!" quite like a pot of tea and little pancakes (also known as flapjacks) fresh from the stove. To make flapjacks, put 1 cup of plain flour in a bowl, and then add ½ cup milk, 1 egg, 2 tablespoons sugar, and ¼ cup melted butter. Beat well to make a smooth batter, and then fry tablespoons of the batter in a little butter or oil until golden brown on both sides. Serve warm with more butter and honey—or fruit preserves.

54

Home Comforts

The Jane Austen quote in this design just lent itself so perfectly to the theme of this book, and I wanted to finish it in a simple way that makes it the perfect gift, door hanging, or other small item. This traditional cottage is based on the many lovely little homes I saw when I lived in England, and it represents the kind of cottage we probably all secretly dream of living in!

Fabric: 28-count china pearl Jobelan by Wichelt (stitched over 2 threads)
Stitch count: 57 wide × 57 high
Approx. stitched size: 4¼ in. (11 cm) square

Cut fabric to measure at least 9 inches (23 cm) square, and then fold in half and count out to start stitching at a suitable point. Wash and lightly press the finished piece, and then cut two pieces of foam core board to measure 7 inches (18 cm) square. Center and stretch the stitched piece over one of the boards; next, fold it to the back and glue it in place. Cover the other board with a suitable piece of cotton fabric, and glue it in place on the back. Glue the two boards together well, right sides facing out, and insert a loop of ribbon at the top center for hanging.

Floss Used for Full Stitches:

Symbol		Strands	Type	Number	Color
	c	2	DMC	152	Shell Pink-MD LT
	I	2	DMC	223	Shell Pink-LT
	n	2	DMC	522	Fern Green
	T	2	DMC	523	Fern Green-LT
	-	2	DMC	822	Beige Gray-LT
	^	2	DMC	926	Gray Green-MD
	(	2	DMC	927	Gray Green-LT
	v	2	DMC	3013	Khaki Green-LT
	s	2	DMC	3022	Brown Gray-MD
	o	2	DMC	3023	Brown Gray-LT
	<	2	DMC	3024	Brown Gray-VY LT
	)	2	DMC	3042	Antique Violet-LT
	L	2	DMC	3046	Yellow Beige-MD
	>	2	DMC	3047	Yellow Beige-LT
	u	2	DMC	3363	Pine Green-MD
	/	2	DMC	3364	Pine Green
	~	2	DMC	3727	Antique Mauve-LT
	1	2	DMC	3863	Mocha Beige-MD
	·	2	DMC	3865	Winter White

Floss Used for Half Stitches:

Symbol		Strands	Type	Number	Color
	◆◆	2	DMC	317	Pewter Gray

Floss Used for French Knots:

Symbol		Strands	Type	Number	Color
	●	1	DMC	3768	Gray Green-DK

Floss Used for Back Stitches:

Symbol		Strands	Type	Number	Color
	———	1	DMC	3363	Pine Green-MD
	———	1	DMC	3768	Gray Green-DK
	———	1	DMC	3863	Mocha Beige-MD

LET ME LIVE IN A HOUSE
by the
SIDE OF THE ROAD
and be a Friend to man

58

House by the Side of the Road

In the kitchen of the house I grew up in, there was a sampler with this saying (attributed to Sam Foss)—not a cross-stitched sampler, but one that was printed on fabric and then stitched with freehand embroidery. My mother made that one (which is sadly long lost), so I created this design in memory of the home where I grew up and the love and warmth that surrounded us there.

Fabric: 32-count café mocha Country French Linen by Wichelt (stitched over two threads)
Stitch count: 115 wide × 93 high
Approx. stitched size: 7½ × 5½ in. (19 × 14 cm)

Cut fabric to measure at least 13 × 10 inches (33 × 25.5 cm), and then fold in half and count out to start stitching at a suitable place. Wash and lightly press the finished piece. This design was framed in an antique brown wooden frame measuring approximately 10 × 8 inches (25.4 × 20.5 cm). The stitched piece was stretched and centered over a piece of foam core board and then inserted into the frame.

Floss Used for Full Stitches:

Symbol		Strands	Type	Number	Color
▪	S	2	DMC	317	Pewter Gray
▪	T	2	DMC	436	Tan
▫	v	2	DMC	437	Tan-LT
▪	L	2	DMC	640	Beige Gray-VY DK
▪	<	2	DMC	642	Beige Gray-DK
▫	u	2	DMC	676	Old Gold-LT
▫	∧	2	DMC	758	Terra Cotta-VY LT
▪	m	2	DMC	3012	Khaki Green-MD
▫	>	2	DMC	3013	Khaki Green-LT
▪	r	2	DMC	3041	Antique Violet-MD
▪	c	2	DMC	3042	Antique Violet-LT
▫	)	2	DMC	3053	Green Gray
▪	a	2	DMC	3363	Pine Green-MD
▪	-	2	DMC	3364	Pine Green
▫	I	2	DMC	3774	Desert Sand-VY LT
▪	o	2	DMC	3778	Terra Cotta-LT
▪	n	2	DMC	3863	Mocha Beige-MD
▪	/	2	DMC	3864	Mocha Beige-LT
▫	(	2	DMC	3865	Winter White

Floss Used for Back Stitches:

Symbol		Strands	Type	Number	Color
▪	────	1	DMC	640	Beige Gray-VY DK
▪	────	1	DMC	642	Beige Gray-DK
▪	────	1	DMC	3363	Pine Green-MD

The Sun at Home

This bright and colorful piece reminds us of the simple pleasures and gifts that our home can bring us every day!

Fabric: 28-count latte Country French Linen by Wichelt (stitched over two threads)
Stitch count: 63 wide × 110 high
Approx. stitched size: 4½ × 8 in. (11.5 × 20.5 cm)

Cut fabric to measure at least 7 × 11 inches (18 × 28 cm), and then fold in half and count out to start stitching at a suitable place. When stitching is complete, wash and lightly press the piece. This design is shown flat and unfinished, but it can be finished in several different ways, such as a framed piece or a cheerful wall hanging for any room.

Floss Used for Full Stitches:

Symbol	Strands	Type	Number	Color
u	2	DMC	30	Violet-Blue
>	2	DMC	415	Pearl Gray
a	2	DMC	522	Fern Green
⅂	2	DMC	524	Fern Green-VY LT
·	2	DMC	644	Beige Gray-MD
<	2	DMC	754	Peach-LT
↑	2	DMC	760	Salmon
o	2	DMC	840	Beige Brown-MD
n	2	DMC	841	Beige Brown-LT
‖	2	DMC	931	Antique Blue-MD
c	2	DMC	932	Antique Blue-LT
0	2	DMC	3023	Brown Gray-LT
1	2	DMC	3024	Brown Gray-VY LT
v	2	DMC	3046	Yellow Beige-MD
m	2	DMC	3047	Yellow Beige-LT
L	2	DMC	3364	Pine Green
/	2	DMC	3713	Salmon-VY LT
)	2	DMC	3823	Yellow-UL Pale
^	2	DMC	3827	Golden Brown-Pale
[(	2	DMC	3855	Autumn Gold-LT
-	2	DMC	3865	Winter White
~	2	DMC	26	Pale Mauve

Floss Used for Half Stitches:

Symbol	Strands	Type	Number	Color
◆◆	2	DMC	414	Steel Gray-DK
·	2	DMC	644	Beige Gray-MD
m	2	DMC	3047	Yellow Beige-LT
/	2	DMC	3713	Salmon-VY LT

Floss Used for Quarter Stitches:

Symbol	Strands	Type	Number	Color
·	2	DMC	644	Beige Gray-MD
c	2	DMC	932	Antique Blue-LT
m	2	DMC	3047	Yellow Beige-LT
/	2	DMC	3713	Salmon-VY LT

Floss Used for Back Stitches:

Symbol	Strands	Type	Number	Color
▬▬▬	1	DMC	930	Antique Blue-DK
▬▬▬	1	DMC	3363	Pine Green-MD
▬▬▬	1	DMC	3787	Brown Gray-DK
▬▬▬	1	DMC	3827	Golden Brown-Pale

Floss Used for Specialty Stitches:

Symbol	Strands	Type	Number	Color
Algerian Eyelet	2	DMC	3827	Golden Brown-Pale

Cavan Images/Cavan via Getty Images

Cottage Seasons

Living with the seasons and their natural rhythms and bounty is very much a part of cottage life; we celebrate the unfolding of the year and incorporate its magic into our everyday lives. These seasonal pieces are a sweet reminder to live in the present and enjoy the moment!

"There is no season such delight can bring . . . as summer, autumn, winter, and the spring."

Anonymous

Time to Bloom

Spring—isn't it just the most beautiful season, full of birdsong, blossoms, and new life? I wanted to create a cottage that was also a very special little birdhouse, in honor of the birds that live all around my home and give me such sweet song and pleasure every day. The soft fabric and pretty colors of this design are the perfect reflection of this season.

Fabric: 28-count star sapphire Jobelan by Wichelt (stitched over two threads)
Stitch count: 57 wide × 97 high
Approx. stitched size: 4 × 7 in. (10 × 18 cm)

Cut fabric to measure at least 8 × 11 inches (20.5 × 28 cm), and then fold in half and count out to start stitching at a suitable point. When stitching is completed, wash and lightly press the work. To present it as shown, trim the sides and bottom of the fabric to 1½ inches (4 cm), and the top to 2½ inches (6.5 cm), and carefully remove any loose threads. Fold over the top by 1 inch (2.5 cm) and press the fold lightly in place. Carefully insert a length of ¼-inch (1.5 cm) ribbon, allowing about 4 inches (10 cm) on each end. Tie a knot for hanging in each end and hold the ribbon in place with a few miniature clothes pegs, as shown in the picture.

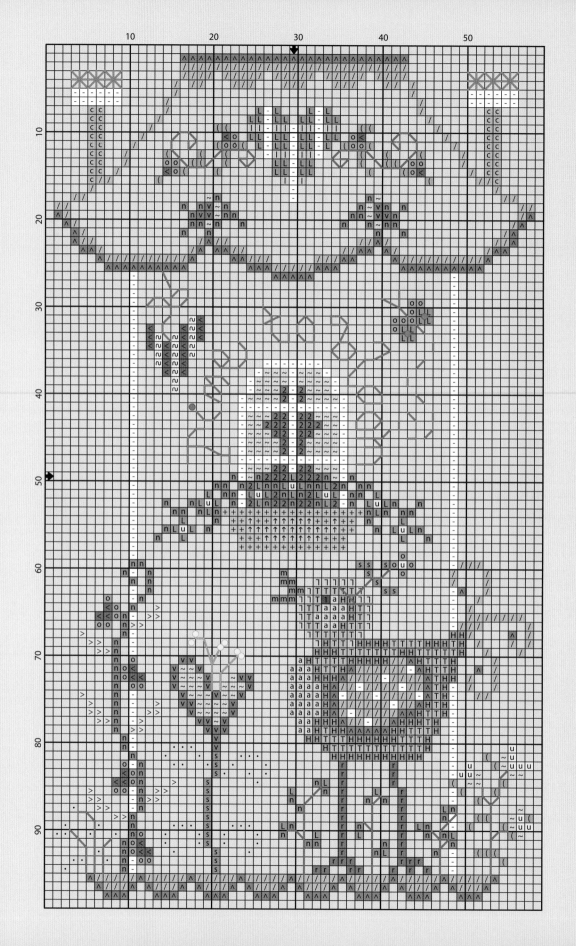

Floss Used for Full Stitches:

	Symbol	Strands	Type	Number	Color
	o	2	DMC	152	Shell Pink-MD LT
	<	2	DMC	223	Shell Pink-LT
	ℕ	2	DMC	225	Shell Pink-UL VY LT
	V	2	DMC	316	Antique Mauve-MD
	m	2	DMC	402	Mahogany-VY LT
	2	2	DMC	414	Steel Gray-DK
	+	2	DMC	437	Tan-LT
	n	2	DMC	522	Fern Green
	>	2	DMC	524	Fern Green-VY LT
	↑	2	DMC	738	Tan-VY LT
	a	2	DMC	754	Peach-LT
	~	2	DMC	778	Antique Mauve-VY LT
	∧	2	DMC	926	Gray Green-MD
	/	2	DMC	927	Gray Green-LT
	s	2	DMC	3012	Khaki Green-MD
	·	2	DMC	3013	Khaki Green-LT
	H	2	DMC	3032	Mocha Brown-MD
	⅂	2	DMC	3033	Mocha Brown-VY LT
	L	2	DMC	3042	Antique Violet-LT
	[(	2	DMC	3364	Pine Green
	∎	2	DMC	3371	Black Brown
	∣	2	DMC	3743	Antique Violet-VY LT
	T	2	DMC	3782	Mocha Brown-LT
	u	2	DMC	3855	Autumn Gold-LT
	r	2	DMC	3859	Rosewood-LT
	c	2	DMC	3864	Mocha Beige-LT
	-	2	DMC	3865	Winter White

Floss Used for French Knots:

	Symbol	Strands	Type	Number	Color
	●	1	DMC	316	Antique Mauve-MD
	○	1	DMC	3855	Autumn Gold-LT
	●	1	DMC	3862	Mocha Beige-DK

Floss Used for Back Stitches:

	Symbol	Strands	Type	Number	Color
	────	1	DMC	3032	Mocha Brown-MD
	────	1	DMC	3363	Pine Green-MD
	────	1	DMC	3862	Mocha Beige-DK

Floss Used for Specialty Stitches:

	Symbol	Strands	Type	Number	Color
	Algerian Eyelet	2	DMC	926	Gray Green-MD

La Vie en Rose

Roses—probably the most beautiful and best loved of all the flowers—
are an essential part of summer! This is a little French-style cottage
stitched in soft shades of pink and green, and it reminds us that life is
truly a gift if we choose to look through the lens of beauty and joy.

Fabric: 28-count china pearl Jobelan by Wichelt (stitched over 2 threads)
Stitch count: 83 wide × 57 high
Approx. stitched size: 6 × 4 in. (15 × 10 cm)

Cut fabric to measure at least 10 × 8 inches (25.5 × 20.5 cm), and then fold in half and count
out to start stitching at a suitable point. When stitching is complete, wash and press lightly.
This piece was mounted in a white antique frame measuring approximately 8 × 6 inches
(20.5 × 15 cm). The stitching was stretched over a piece of foam core board that fits within
the frame's aperture and held in place on the back with glue or tape before being inserted
into the frame. A few little fabric roses were glued onto the top left of the frame, but this
step is optional.

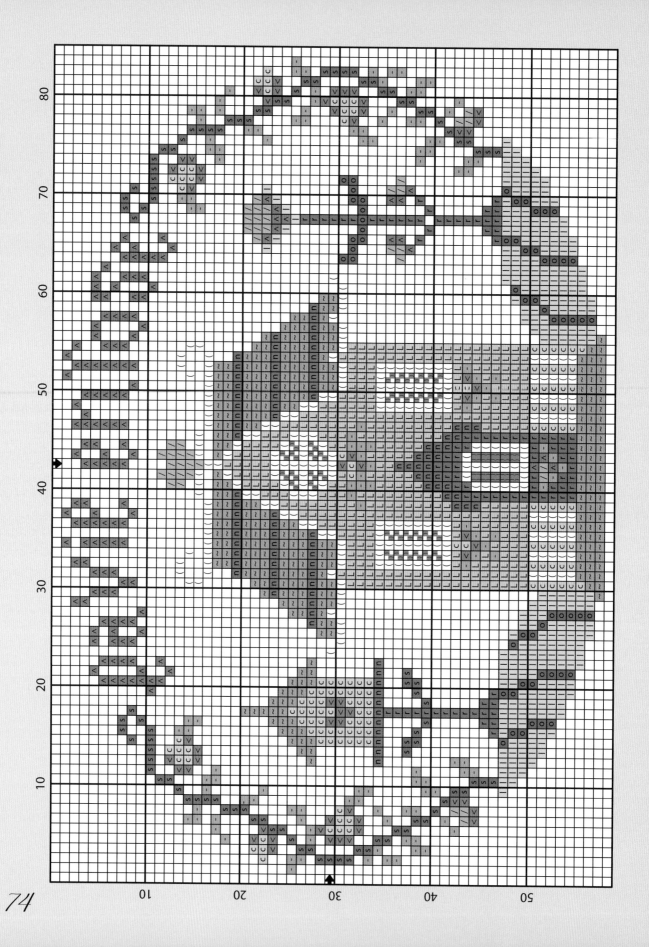

Floss Used for Full Stitches:

Symbol		Strands	Type	Number	Color
■	s	2	DMC	320	Pistachio Green-MD
■	-	2	DMC	368	Pistachio Green-LT
■	o	2	DMC	502	Blue Green
■	n	2	DMC	646	Beaver Gray-DK
■	~	2	DMC	647	Beaver Gray-MD
■	L	2	DMC	842	Beige Brown-VY LT
■	<	2	DMC	962	Dusty Rose-MD
■	c	2	DMC	963	Dusty Rose-UL VY LT
■	^	2	DMC	3688	Mauve-MD
■	/	2	DMC	3689	Mauve-LT
■	l	2	DMC	3813	Blue Green-LT
■	r	2	DMC	3862	Mocha Beige-DK
□	((	2	DMC	3865	Winter White

Floss Used for Half Stitches:

Symbol		Strands	Type	Number	Color
■	))	2	DMC	414	Steel Gray-DK

Helin Loik-Tomson/iStock/Getty Images Plus via Getty Images

Even if you don't grow roses yourself, you can still enjoy the sweetness of these immortal blooms by always keeping a bottle of rose essential oil on hand—or burning rose incense. You can also make a simple potpourri by combining dried rose petals, lavender leaves and blossoms, and some thyme or rosemary leaves. Spread in a glass bowl, add the finely grated peel of one lemon and one orange, as well as a few dried cloves. Sprinkle with rose essential oil and stir the flower mixture well. This product will keep for quite a while and impart a gentle fragrance to your bedroom or living room.

78

Welcome to Our Patch!

I can just imagine two friendly little ghosts setting up home in a pumpkin cottage! This is a fun piece to stitch for Halloween or just as an autumn decoration.

Fabric: 28-count beautiful beige linen by Wichelt (stitched over two threads)
Stitch count: 68 wide × 68 high
Approx. stitched size: 5 in. (13 cm) in diameter

Cut fabric to measure at least 11 inches (28 cm) in diameter, and then fold in half and count out to start stitching at a suitable point. When stitching is complete, wash and press lightly. This design was finished in an 8-inch (20.5-cm) wooden hoop; the fabric was cut about 1½ inches (4 cm) larger in diameter than the hoop, as was a piece of cotton backing fabric. They were then placed into the hoop with the stitched piece on top and centered before the screws were tightened and colorful ribbons were attached for hanging.

WELCOME TO OUR PATCH!

Floss Used for Full Stitches:

Symbol	Strands	Type	Number	Color
/	2	DMC	02	Lightest Gray
I	2	DMC	352	Coral-LT
((	2	DMC	353	Peach
%	2	DMC	413	Pewter Gray-DK
o	2	DMC	414	Steel Gray-DK
c	2	DMC	434	Brown-LT
∧	2	DMC	436	Tan
<	2	DMC	611	Drab Brown
-	2	DMC	676	Old Gold-LT
L	2	DMC	727	Topaz-VY LT
n	2	DMC	3012	Khaki Green-MD
~	2	DMC	3013	Khaki Green-LT
◆◆	2	DMC	3363	Pine Green-MD
v	2	DMC	3364	Pine Green
∞	2	DMC	3778	Terra Cotta-LT
r	2	DMC	3835	Grape-MD
))	2	DMC	3836	Grape-LT
·	2	DMC	White	White

Floss Used for Half Stitches:

Symbol	Strands	Type	Number	Color
L	2	DMC	727	Topaz-VY LT

Floss Used for French Knots:

Symbol	Strands	Type	Number	Color
○	1	DMC	3013	Khaki Green-LT

Floss Used for Back Stitches:

Symbol	Strands	Type	Number	Color
——	1	DMC	413	Pewter Gray-DK
——	1	DMC	3012	Khaki Green-MD
——	1	DMC	3363	Pine Green-MD

Autumn would not be complete without pumpkins, of course. Why not try making this easy and delicious pumpkin soup after a frosty evening of trick or treat? Peel and chop a medium pumpkin, onion, and large potato. Place these pieces in a large saucepan and cover with lots of good vegetable stock or broth and a good sprinkling of ground pepper and dried paprika. Simmer until the vegetables are very soft, and then mash the mixture in a blender or food processor until thick and smooth; reheat gently before serving, and top with a spoonful of sour cream or plain yogurt and lots of fresh parsley.

Our Winter Home

Band samplers have always been one of my favorite things to design, and this classic style design incorporates so many of the good things of winter and the holiday season—even down to a little wise owl reminding us to enjoy every moment of this special time.

Fabric: 28-count lambswool Jobelan by Wichelt (stitched over 2 threads)
Stitch count: 55 wide × 125 high
Approx. stitched size: 4 × 9 in. (10 × 23 cm)

Cut fabric to measure at least 7 × 12 inches (18 × 30.5 cm), and then fold in half and count out to start stitching at a suitable point. Wash and lightly press the finished stitching, and then cut a piece of foam core board (or similar artist's board) measuring approximately 6 × 12 inches (15 × 30.5 cm). Center and stretch the stitched piece over the board, and fold the excess fabric to the back, holding it firmly in place with tape or glue. A little red gingham bow was attached to the top left of the piece, but this step is optional.

86

Floss Used for Full Stitches:

Symbol		Strands	Type	Number	Color
■	C	2	DMC	223	Shell Pink-LT
■	∧	2	DMC	320	Pistachio Green-MD
■	1	2	DMC	356	Terra Cotta-MD
□	~	2	DMC	415	Pearl Gray
■	⊠	2	DMC	435	Brown-VY LT
□	u	2	DMC	436	Tan
■	)	2	DMC	502	Blue Green
■	#	2	DMC	611	Drab Brown
■	L	2	DMC	676	Old Gold-LT
□	<	2	DMC	677	Old Gold-VY LT
■	>	2	DMC	729	Old Gold-MD
■	n	2	DMC	926	Gray Green-MD
■	I	2	DMC	927	Gray Green-LT
■	v	2	DMC	3032	Mocha Brown-MD
■	o	2	DMC	3722	Shell Pink-MD
■	T	2	DMC	3778	Terra Cotta-LT
■	(	2	DMC	3782	Mocha Brown-LT
■	/	2	DMC	3813	Blue Green-LT
□	-	2	DMC	3865	Winter White

Floss Used for French Knots:

Symbol		Strands	Type	Number	Color
■	●	1	DMC	535	Ash Gray-VY LT
■	●	1	DMC	3722	Shell Pink-MD
■	●	1	DMC	3768	Gray Green-DK

Floss Used for Back Stitches:

Symbol		Strands	Type	Number	Color
■	━━━	1	DMC	367	Pistachio Green-DK
■	━━━	1	DMC	535	Ash Gray-VY LT
■	━━━	1	DMC	611	Drab Brown
■	━━━	1	DMC	729	Old Gold-MD
■	━━━	1	DMC	3768	Gray Green-DK

Snow Globe Cottage

Snow globes are such an iconic symbol of both winter and the holidays, and this little stitched piece echoes all the warmth and charm of snow globes, in stitched form. It's quick and easy to stitch and would make a charming addition to cottage winter decorating or a holiday tree.

Fabric: 28-count star sapphire Jobelan by Wichelt (stitched over two threads)
Stitch count: 71 wide × 68 high
Approx. stitched size: 5¼ × 5 in. (13.5 × 13 cm)

Cut fabric to measure at least 9 × 8 inches (23 × 20.5 cm), and then fold in half and count out to begin stitching at a suitable point. Wash and lightly press the finished stitching. Cut a piece of foam core board (or similar) that measures 6½ × 5½ inches (16.5 × 14 cm), and then center and stretch the embroidery over it. Tape or glue it firmly to the back of the board. Cut another larger piece of board approximately 8¼ × 6 inches (21 × 15 cm) and cover with suitable cotton holiday fabric, holding it in place at the back with tape or glue. Center the stitched piece on the backing board, and glue it firmly in place; add a decorative heart button at top center, if desired.

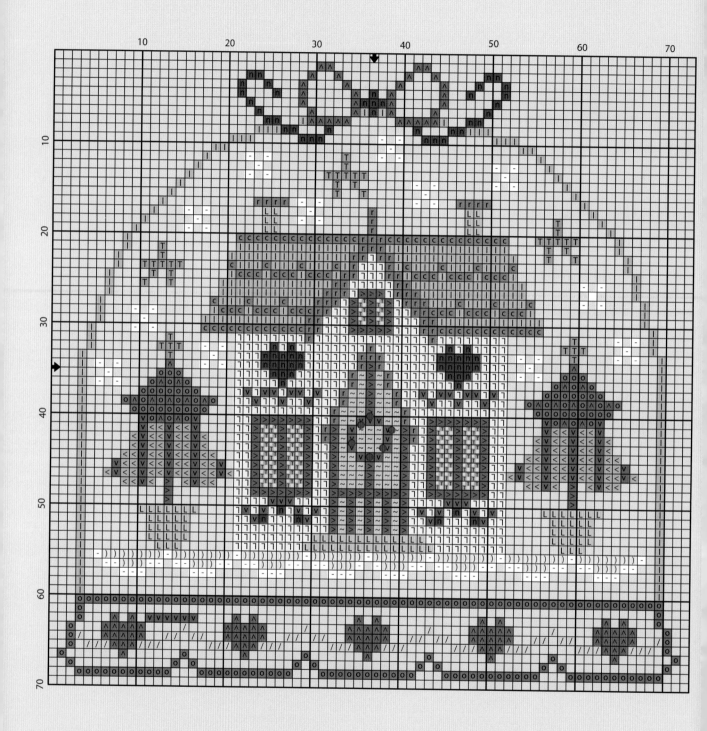

Floss Used for Full Stitches:

Symbol		Strands	Type	Number	Color
	)	2	DMC	02	Lightest Gray
	I	2	DMC	03	Med Lightest Gray
	c	2	DMC	04	Medium Steel Grey
	v	2	DMC	163	Celadon Green-MD
	^	2	DMC	223	Shell Pink-LT
	L	2	DMC	437	Tan-LT
	o	2	DMC	502	Blue Green
	T	2	DMC	729	Old Gold-MD
	>	2	DMC	840	Beige Brown-MD
	~	2	DMC	842	Beige Brown-VY LT
	r	2	DMC	926	Gray Green-MD
	⌐	2	DMC	928	Gray Green-VY LT
	n	2	DMC	3722	Shell Pink-MD
	<	2	DMC	3816	Celadon Green-MD
	/	2	DMC	3817	Celadon Green-LT
	-	2	DMC	White	White

Floss Used for Half Stitches:

Symbol		Strands	Type	Number	Color
	T	2	DMC	729	Old Gold-MD

Floss Used for French Knots:

Symbol		Strands	Type	Number	Color
	●	1	DMC	3722	Shell Pink-MD

Cottage Seasons

This is a small quilt-style, stitched piece that reminds us of the beauty to be found through the year; four little cottages are surrounded by tiny floral and leaf borders for each season. The cottages and borders could also be stitched individually as tiny pillows or box tops.

Fabric: 28-count china pearl Jobelan by Wichelt (stitched over 2 threads)
Stitch count: 85 wide × 85 high
Approx. stitched size: 6 in. (15 cm) square

Cut fabric to measure at least 10 inches (25.5 cm) square, and then fold in half and count out to start stitching at a suitable point. Wash and lightly press the finished stitching, and trim the fabric to measure 1½ inches (4 cm) beyond the stitching at the sides and bottom, 2½ inches (6.5 cm) at the top (for the fold). Fold the top down by 1 inch (2.5 cm), and press it in place. Insert a length of ¼-inch (0.5 cm) ribbon, allowing it to extend 3 to 4 inches (7.5 to 10 cm) at each side, and tie a loop knot in each end. Insert the ribbon through the fold, and hold it in place with miniature clothes pegs, as shown in the photo.

Floss Used for Full Stitches:

Symbol		Strands	Type	Number	Color
	+	2	DMC	320	Pistachio Green-MD
	⋈	2	DMC	414	Steel Gray-DK
	~	2	DMC	437	Tan-LT
	I	2	DMC	522	Fern Green
	/	2	DMC	524	Fern Green-VY LT
	∷	2	DMC	611	Drab Brown
	9	2	DMC	642	Beige Gray-DK
	∧	2	DMC	644	Beige Gray-MD
	>	2	DMC	676	Old Gold-LT
	<	2	DMC	677	Old Gold-VY LT
	0	2	DMC	738	Tan-VY LT
	v	2	DMC	758	Terra Cotta-VY LT
	n	2	DMC	760	Salmon
	-	2	DMC	822	Beige Gray-LT
	a	2	DMC	932	Antique Blue-LT
	⅂	2	DMC	950	Desert Sand-LT
	s	2	DMC	3032	Mocha Brown-MD
	c	2	DMC	3041	Antique Violet-MD
	(	2	DMC	3042	Antique Violet-LT
	u	2	DMC	3046	Yellow Beige-MD
	7	2	DMC	3047	Yellow Beige-LT
	o	2	DMC	3328	Salmon-DK
	)	2	DMC	3348	Yellow Green-LT
	↑	2	DMC	3364	Pine Green
	1	2	DMC	3713	Salmon-VY LT
	T	2	DMC	3778	Terra Cotta-LT
	2	2	DMC	3782	Mocha Brown-LT
	L	2	DMC	3813	Blue Green-LT
	H	2	DMC	3828	Hazelnut Brown

Floss Used for Back Stitches:

Symbol		Strands	Type	Number	Color
	———	1	DMC	611	Drab Brown
	———	1	DMC	3347	Yellow Green-MD
	———	1	DMC	3363	Pine Green-MD

"His house was perfect, whether
you liked food, or sleep,
or work, or storytelling, or singing,
or a pleasant mixture of them all."
J. R. R. Tolkien, The Hobbit

(Sounds like the perfect cottage to me!)

CHARTING AND ALPHABETS TO CREATE YOUR OWN DESIGNS

A dapting existing cross-stitch patterns or creating your own with words or sayings that are particularly meaningful to you is not difficult and is wonderfully rewarding. The designs in this book are such that many of them can be adapted in various ways, starting with the colors used. If you don't like the colors in a particular design, simply swap them out for ones that you prefer. (Just remember to keep the general depth of color in mind—darker shades and paler ones, as needed.)

If you wish to create your own sayings, it is possible to get several charting systems that make this process a breeze. I have used Patternmaker for Cross Stitch (a program by HobbyWare) for many years now and find it very easy and user friendly—but, of course, you may find another favorite.

Alternatively, most of my designs start life in the old-fashioned way, with a pencil, colored pens or markers, an eraser (very important!), and lots of graph paper. First, choose the count of the fabric you are going to use (28-count = 14 stitches to the inch; 32-count = 16 stitches to the inch). Work out how much space you are going to need for your chosen words/saying, and then measure this area out on the graph paper. Use a pencil to lightly sketch the words/quote in this space. Then fill in the blocks with lettering of your choice. You can use any of the ideas given in this book or the additional alphabet charts. Or you can make up your own lettering, as I generally do—there are no rules. Sometimes a word/saying is centered on the graph, and other times it is randomly placed down or across the piece, as you will see from the different designs in this book.

Do remember that writing in whole stitches is generally done in a paler shade of floss than backstitch lettering, which is done in a single strand of floss and thus needs a darker or more intense color to stand out.

If you wish to change the words/quotes on any of the existing designs in this book, first photocopy the chart, enlarging it if necessary. Then cut a piece of squared/graph paper to cover the existing words, glue it down, and fill in the words of your choice.

Happy stitching and creating!

Floss Used for Full Stitches:

Symbol		Strands	Type	Number	Color
	o	2	DMC	931	Antique Blue-MD
	-	2	DMC	932	Antique Blue-LT

Floss Used for French Knots:

Symbol		Strands	Type	Number	Color
	●	1	DMC	931	Antique Blue-MD

Floss Used for Back Stitches:

Symbol		Strands	Type	Number	Color
	▬▬▬	1	DMC	931	Antique Blue-MD

Note:
Fabric varies according to the design being stitched.

VISUAL INDEX

Cottage Garden Quilt 3

Apple Crisp Cake 7

My Cottage Kitchen 11

Wool and Whimsy Cottage 15

Little House on Wheels 21

Cottage Cakery 25

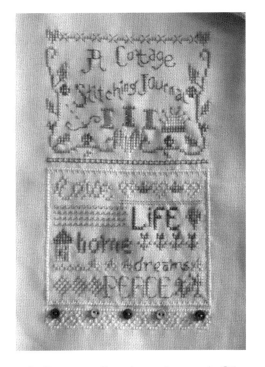

A Cottage Stitching Journal 31

House by the Sea 35

Cottage Joy Mandala 41

Little House . . . 45

Welcome Home 49

Home Comforts 55

House by the Side of the Road 59

The Sun at Home 63

Time to Bloom 69

La Vie en Rose 73

Welcome to Our Patch! 79

Our Winter Home 85

Snow Globe Cottage 91

Cottage Seasons 95